I Can Read About™

CREATURES OF THE NIGHT

Written by David Cutts • Illustrated by Janice Kinnealy

Consultant: Kathy Carlstead, Ph.D., National Zoological Park, Smithsonian Institution

It's a beautiful day! The sun is shining.
Birds are singing. Bees are buzzing.
Butterflies fly from flower to flower.
Chipmunks scamper for nuts and seeds.
All day long, many animals
are busy.

But as the sun dips below the trees and darkness falls on the fields and forests, the animals of the daytime settle down to sleep for the night.

Now the moon is out, and the stars are twinkling. The
animals of the day are silent. But if you listen closely, you can
hear something else.

Can you hear the creatures of the night?

Some of them move along the ground. Others climb in the trees. Still others fly through the air. These special creatures are called nocturnal (nock-TER-nil) animals. *Nocturnal* means "of the night." Just as their name suggests, nocturnal animals are active at night.

Let's explore the world of night creatures. Are any insects active at night? The firefly, or lightning bug, is. Fireflies are easy to see when it is dark. Special chemicals mix inside their bodies as they fly. These chemicals make a light inside the firefly. Fireflies find their mates by blinking these lights.

Many moths are creatures of the night. These insects are easy to see when they fly near bright lights. Moths are related to butterflies. But when the sun goes down and many butterflies rest, most moths are active. For example, certain hawk moths fly about, searching for flowers that bloom at night.

Hawk moth

The hawk moth looks for the sweet nectar found in the flowers. Using its long, tubelike tongue—which works something like a straw—the moth sips the nectar. This special tongue is called a *proboscis* (prah-BAH-sis). When the moth's proboscis is not being used, it is curled up like a spring.

Moths have big eyes and *antennae* (an-TEN-ee) on their heads. Some male moths use their antennae to smell female moths. A male luna moth can smell the scent of his mate even when she is miles away.

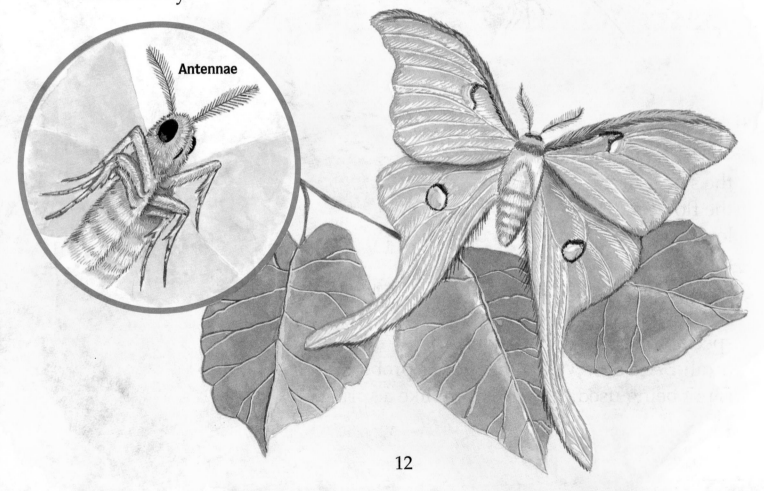

Antennae

Many moths would make
tasty dinners for the spiders,
frogs, and lizards that hunt at
night. That is why moths often
have dull brown or gray wings
to help them hide in the dark.

13

Some of the strangest creatures of the night are bats. These special mammals are the only animals in the world that have both wings and fur. Many animals have fur, but they do not have wings.

14

Many insects have wings, but they do not have fur. And birds have wings, but they have feathers instead of fur.

15

Wing membrane

Tail membrane

A bat's wings are made of a very thin, soft skin called a membrane. This membrane stretches between the bones of the fingers and between the bat's legs and arm bones. Most bats also have a tail membrane. It stretches between the bat's legs.

Bats use the claws on their feet to hang upside down. That's how they sleep during the day. Some sleep in caves. Others sleep in trees or in empty buildings. Sometimes bats sleep in attics. At night they fly outside to hunt for food.

Bats in cave

Most bats eat fruit as well as the insects that fly at night, such as mosquitoes, moths, and gnats. Bats catch these insects as they fly through the air. A bat uses its wings like a broom. It sweeps an insect into its tail membrane. Then it bends its head down and eats the insect.

To take a drink, a bat flies low over a pond or lake. It skims the surface of the water with its lower jaw.

Bats have tiny eyes and poor eyesight. Yet they are excellent fliers. How do they fly at night without bumping into things? They use something called *echolocation* (eh-koh-low-KAY-shun).

Here is how it works. A bat has large ears to help it hear very well. As the bat flies, it makes special sounds. People cannot hear these sounds, but the bat can. Each sound bounces off a flying insect or other object, and an echo comes back. The bat hears the echoes and knows exactly where the insect or object is. That's why bats are such good fliers. They can find their way around on the darkest nights.

Many other night animals also have large ears, so they can hear what they do not see. For example, mice cannot see well, but they have large ears and excellent hearing to help them escape hungry enemies. Mice also have long whiskers. They use their whiskers to help them feel their way around in the dark as they search for food.

In fields and forests, most mice eat seeds, grain, plant stems, and roots. These creatures dig down into the ground to build their nests. Then they line the nests with soft grass.

The grasshopper mouse lives in the desert or prairie. It makes its home in an old burrow that may have been dug by a prairie dog or a gopher.

Grasshopper mice like to eat animals instead of plants. They search for worms, scorpions, and other small creatures of the night. But they get their name from their favorite food— grasshoppers!

Many other animals that live in the desert or the prairie are creatures of the night. That is because during the day it is too hot to move around searching for food. So pocket mice and kangaroo rats curl up in their cool burrows below the ground.

Here and there a ground squirrel pokes its head up out of its burrow. Sleepy lizards and snakes move from the hot sun into the shade of a rock to keep cool.

Kangaroo rat

Silky pocket mouse

But as the sun goes down and the temperature drops, the desert comes alive. A pocket mouse steals out, looking for seeds. Soon the fur-lined pouches on the outside of its cheeks are full of food, so it scampers back down to its underground storeroom.

Kangaroo rats are also active at night. They hop around on their hind legs, just like tiny kangaroos. When they have to, they can jump 7 feet (2 meters) or more in one hop!

Ground squirrels are out, too, gathering nuts
and grain. They also chase after insects and mice.
But if a coyote comes looking for a meal, the
ground squirrels hurry into their homes. There
they are safe from coyotes, foxes, and owls—but
not from predators such as snakes and badgers.

A hungry badger can dig down into the burrows of ground squirrels, pocket mice, and kangaroo rats. This excellent hunter uses the large, strong claws on its front feet to dig very quickly.

Snakes also prey upon ground squirrels and prairie dogs. The snake is thin enough to slither down inside these animals' burrows.

Owls are well-suited to hunting during the night.

In the desert, these birds may make their homes in hollowed-out cactus plants. In the forest, owls roost, or settle down to rest, in trees. Their brownish-gray feathers blend in very well with the trees' branches and trunk.

When night comes, the owls awaken, ready to hunt. Their big eyes can spot a mouse, rabbit, or squirrel on the darkest night. The owl swoops down and grabs its prey in its sharp talons, or claws. The bird's soft feathers make very little noise, allowing the owl to surprise its prey. Back in its nest, the owl uses its curved beak for ripping and tearing apart its meal. Owls gulp down their prey—feathers, fur, bones, and all.

There are many kinds of owls. The smallest is the elf owl. It is only about the size of your hand. It lives in hot desert lands.

Elf owl

The largest is the gray owl. It can stretch out its wings farther than you can stretch your arms. It lives in the forests of Alaska and Canada.

Gray owl

Did
you ever try
to fool someone
by "playing
possum"? We get
this saying from a
creature of the night
called the opossum.
When the opossum is
afraid, it sometimes rolls
over as if it were dead.
After its enemy is gone,
the opossum awakens. It
climbs a tree to find a safe spot.
Opossums are very comfortable in
trees—they can even grasp branches
with their tails like a monkey.

A mother opossum keeps her babies with her all the time when they are first born. The newborn opossums are very tiny and helpless. They stay in their mother's pouch. Later, they ride on her back. Finally, they are strong enough to walk and climb and search for food. They eat fruit, nuts, and tender plants.

This night animal looks like a walking pincushion. It's the porcupine, and its body is covered with long, stiff quills. Each quill has tiny sharp hooks on the end. If a coyote, wolf, or lynx gets too close, it gets stuck with the porcupine's quills. Porcupines sleep during the day in holes in the ground or between rocks. At night they climb into evergreen trees to eat the tender bark.

Skunks eat different kinds of food. They roam through the woodlands at night looking for insects, fruit, small furry animals, eggs, nuts, and grass. Their favorite food is caterpillars.

Sometimes a skunk is annoyed by someone or something. When this happens, the skunk raises its tail. Then it stamps its front feet. If this warning is ignored, the skunk lets out a foul smell. That's enough to chase anyone away!

Beavers cannot protect themselves with strong odors or sharp quills or by playing possum. Instead, they build special houses where they are safe from their enemies. All night long they work and build. Beavers use their sharp teeth to gnaw through trees.

They build a dam to make a pond. In the middle of the pond they build their house. It is called a lodge. It has an underwater entrance to help keep visitors out. But the beavers can swim in and out easily. With their webbed feet and flat tails, they are at home in the water.

Crash! Bang! Who's out there by the garbage cans? It's those midnight thieves—the raccoons! These clever animals use their paws like hands. They quickly learn how to open garbage-can covers in order to find scraps of food.

A mother raccoon teaches her babies how to find worms, insects, turtle eggs, and berries. She shows them how to catch tadpoles, fish, frogs, and salamanders to eat. The curious babies like to explore wherever they can under the cover of darkness.

When the sun rises, the raccoons are gone. All the creatures of the night seem to have vanished. By the time you wake up, they are already sound asleep for another day.

But when darkness comes again, the animals of the night will be back . . . creeping and climbing, swooping and flying. They will slither and scurry, looking for something to eat. So if you hear a sound in the middle of the night, take a peek out your window.

Who knows what
fascinating creatures
are out there?